QUIET EMBERS
A Poetry of Faith

KELLEY MORRIS

Raw Earth Ink

2024

This book is a work of poetry.

Copyright 2024 by Kelley Morris

All rights reserved. No part of this book may be reproduced or used in any manner without express written permission from the author except in the case of quotations used in a book review in which a clear link to the source of the quote and its author is required.

First paperback edition July 2024

Cover art by Ryan Morris
Interior design by tara caribou

ISBN 978-1-960991-30-0 (paperback)

Published by Raw Earth Ink
PO Box 39332
Ninilchik, AK 99639
www.raw-earth-ink.com

*For Dad.
You were a peaceful man
of quiet strength and deep faith.
I miss you.*

He drew me closer to His side.
I sought His will to know.
And in that will, I now abide.
Wherever He leads, I'll go.

—

"Wherever He Leads, I'll Go"
B.B. McKinney

DUSTY WORKBOOTS

You covered
So much ground
On the journey
Mile after mile
Your heart
Prepared
To listen
Your feet
Willing
To move-
In times of doubt
Trusting
The Love
That securely
Held your soul-
I can see you now
Sharing that Love
As you carefully
Unlace and remove
Dusty workboots
Graciously
Handing them
To another
Confident
Your steps
Would continue
To be protected
As would your heart

*...speak to one another with psalms, hymns, and songs from the Spirit.
Sing and make music from your heart to the Lord.*

—

Ephesians 5:19

INTO THE LIGHT

So many matters
Remain unseen
Hidden in the
Day-to-day
Heartaches
Self-doubt
And sorrow
Masked by smiles
Forced upon faces
At the very last second
To avert any danger
Of two people
Recognizing
Shared feelings
Mutual difficulties-
Would allowing a tear to fall bring peace?
Perhaps…as it joins
Those already fallen
Into the sea
Those already fallen
Into the beauty
Of a place where
Heartache and happiness
Peacefully coexist

*I once was lost, but now am found.
Was blind, but now I see.*

—

"Amazing Grace"
John Newton

ALREADY THERE

Walking through
A dark tunnel
Walls moving
Closer together
With each step
Fear grabs hold
But I pull away
Remembering
Your promise-
Not for wealth
Not for success
No, a promise
That no matter
Where the next
Step takes me
You are there
Even if I forget
Even if I ignore
You will not walk away-
You cannot walk away-
You are the light
At the end
Of the tunnel

*Because Thy promise, I believe.
O Lamb of God, I come.*

"Just As I Am"
Charlotte Elliott

RESTFUL REMINDER

Wars of the mind
Not easily recognized
Or understood
Even though felt
In every fiber
Of this body-
Shaking legs
Tapping fingers
Aching temples-
Hurried thoughts
Fighting over
Which is most
Formidable
Palpable fear
Of what will happen
If the wrong one escapes-
Suddenly
Interrupted by
A restful reminder-
Let go...allow each
Hurried thought
To escape
See the ones
Long hidden
For what they are-
Mistakes, not definitions
Let them float away
Forever forgiven
Forever forgotten

There is no shadow of turning with Thee.

"Great is Thy Faithfulness"
Thomas Obadiah Chisholm

SURROUNDED

Sun shines bright
On a new morning
Offering the chance
For a fresh start-

Please don't
Turn away
I need to see more
Than your shadow

Shadows
Only show a glimpse
Distorted at best
Of the truth
Of the beauty

Let me live
In the middle
Of your love
Not on the edges
Of your shadow

*Can we find a friend so faithful,
Who will all our sorrows share?*

—

"What a Friend We Have in Jesus"
Joseph M. Scriven

THE ANSWER

What is joy?
Is it a state of being
Based on circumstances?
Claimed as one of
My greatest desires
Yet, it often eludes
As I seek to control
Everything
Within reach

Could the answer be so simple?

I don't understand...
Trusting that You
My faithful friend
Will carry my worries
And once I give them over
Will flood my soul with joy

*In seasons of distress and grief,
My soul has often found relief.*

—

"Sweet Hour of Prayer"
William W. Walford

SWEET PEACE

My mind will
Hardly let me
Read the words
Without also
Singing the notes
Melody and lyrics
Interwoven
In my memories
In seasons of distress and grief
I can hear
The simple phrase
Playing in my mind-
Hospital waiting rooms
Lying on an MRI table
Waiting for a phone call
Sitting at a funeral-
Why these times?
Why these words?
Why this melody?
My soul has often found relief
Listen closely
Can you hear
The perfectly
Peaceful
Resolution

*Angels descending bring from above,
echoes of mercy, whispers of love.*

—

"Blessed Assurance"
Fanny Crosby

COCOON

I have never seen
An angel here
On this earth
But I have felt
Their presence
Permanent imprints
Remain etched
On my life
On my heart
Messages of mercy
Messages of love
In times when
All else seemed
Frightening
And uncertain
Circumstances
Threatening
To overtake
Mind, body, and soul
Angels grabbed hold
Wrapping me safely
Inside a cocoon
Protecting me from
The outside world
Until once again
I was able
To rest
To trust
To love

Mercy there was great, and grace was free.

—

"At Calvary"
William R. Newell

FREELY GIVEN

Pride is a
Sneaky trap
Often disguised
As happy confidence
It sweetly calls
Barely above
A whisper
Look at you
You are better than her
Better than him
Life cannot be
Only about self
No, it surely
Must be about
Seeing others
Thru the lens
Of mercy and grace
Freely given
By the One
Who loves me
No matter what
Leaving no room
For comparisons

*For in death as in life
You will whisper Your peace to my soul.*

—

"It is Well with My Soul"
Horatio G. Spafford

MEASURED ASSURANCE

Seeking peace
Avoiding sorrow
Seems a logical pursuit
But can sorrow be avoided?
Not if I live long enough-
Drops of sadness
Sprinkle some days
Waves of grief
Crash over others
What about peace?
Sometimes it flows
Gracefully
In the smallest
Of streams
Weaving in
And around
The rocks left behind.
By crashing waves-
Not washing them away
Filtering and polishing
With measured assurance
Leaving behind smooth stones
Of beauty and strength
Waiting to be
Thoughtfully
Picked up
Gently held
Forever treasured

*He will cover you with his feathers,
and under his wings you will find refuge.*

—

Psalm 91:4

*For He will command his angels
concerning you
To guard you in all your ways.*

—

Psalm 91:11

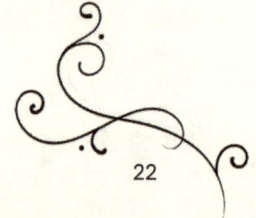

STANDING WATCH

One single feather
All on its own
Light and airy
Soft, comforting
Lining the nest
Of hatchlings
Providing a pillow
For their unsteady
Little heads
Where was this feather before?
It has not always served alone
Maybe it belonged to
The mother bird
Attached to her wings
One of many, together
Creating the power of flight
Strength to carry all things
Needed to provide for
And protect her young
Or maybe it fell from
The wings of an angel
Though unseen
Standing watch
Over the birds
Providing shelter
For my heart

See, on the portals,
he's waiting and watching.
Watching for you and for me

—

"Softly and Tenderly"
Will L. Thompson

CALLING MY NAME

Water was rising
Alongside fear
Threatening to take
Control of the day
As it covered first
Feet, then ankles,
And knees before
Briefly pausing
At the waist-
Desperate
To find a way
Out of the deep
Before suffocation
Reached the chest,
I closed my eyes-
Letting go of worry
Hope began to flow
Along with it-trust
Pushing and pulling
Through the currents
Inch by inch until
My feet stood
Once again
On the shore
Greeted by the love
That never stopped
Calling my name

*Proclaim good news to the poor...
Proclaim freedom for the prisoners and
recovery of sight for the blind.
Set the oppressed free...proclaim the year
of the Lord's favor.*

—

Luke 4:18-19

WILLINGLY

Certain conditions
Hard to imagine
Circumstances
I've never known-
Hunger
Loneliness
Isolation
Oh, I've experienced
Temporary loneliness
But never isolation
Never hunger
Never oppression
Many others have
Many others are
Right at this moment
Too numerous to count
Would I choose those circumstances?
Most assuredly, no
But there is one
Who willingly chose
He offers
Light and love
Freedom and rest
Forgiveness and hope

*Love your enemies,
do good to those who hate you.
Bless those who curse you.
Pray for those who mistreat you.*

—

Luke 6:27-29

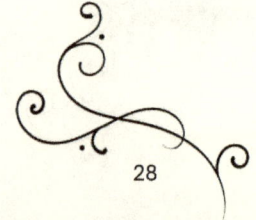

CHOOSE CAREFULLY

If I had to speak
One of two words
Bless or curse
Which would I choose?
Surely it would be the first-
Who wants to leave another
Feeling cursed
Forgotten
Left out
Less-than
No one, I imagine
But if my mouth
Says *bless you*
My heart and actions
Must agree-
Bless is decidedly
Easier to say
But is it easier to achieve?
Speaking one
Cancels the other
Resulting in
Inevitable action
One way or the other-
May my feelings
Words and deeds
Harmonize
Tempered always
With grace

You hem me in behind and before,
And you lay your hand upon me.

—

Psalm 139:5

RENEWED

I can see my mom
Gently folding the edge
Of a cloth napkin
A needle piercing
In even spaces
Crafting tiny holes
For a thread to weave
Over and under
Giving the fabric
A new strength
A renewed purpose-
Hem me in
Fold in my
Rough edges
Sewing a seam of hope
The stitches may hurt
But they will heal
Giving my heart
A new strength
A renewed purpose

Little ones to him belong.
They are weak, but he is strong.

—

"Jesus Loves Me"
Anna B. Warner

CHILDLIKE

When I was a child
Faith was simple
Jesus loves me
This I know
Easily accepted truth
In memorable words
And sweet melody
Sung again and again
Until the seed
Planted in my heart
Began to grow-
But growing
Brought questions
And somehow fear
Became one of the answers
One that threatened
To dig up that seed
And replace it with
Pits of doubt-
As if anything I had done
Could remove me
From the center
Of that love-
Nothing I had done
Placed me there
To begin with-
Time heals some wounds
And faith is a journey
Honest answers to
Sincere questions
Are better understood
Yes, Jesus loves me
The Bible tells me so

*Touched by a loving heart,
wakened by kindness,
chords that were broken
will vibrate once more.*

—

"Rescue the Perishing"
Fanny Crosby

RELEASED

Dissonance
Holds power
To keep hurts
Buried deep
Hearts broken
By what lies
In the past
Long after
Memories
Have faded
Holding
Harmonies
Hostage
From hearing
From feeling
From singing-
Alive, yet
Sleeping-
The power
Of kindness
Releases tension
When paired
With the love
And grace of
The Shepherd
Waking the soul
To hear, feel, sing
Waking the soul
To live in peace

All other ground is sinking sand.

"The Solid Rock"
Edward Mote

UNMOVING

Standing in
Soft sand
Feels good
On my feet
But what happens
When a storm
Approaches?
Do I remain
On the sand
Uncertain
Afraid it will
Quickly wash
From under
My feet
Or do I move
To solid ground
Standing
Securely
On the rock
That promises
To remain strong
That calls to me
Thru the waves
Come, stand here
I will never move

As iron sharpens iron, so one person sharpens another.

—

Proverbs 27:17

PEELING LAYERS

Layers
Upon layers
Upon layers
Potatoes
Carrots
Onions
Each must lose
One of its layers
To fulfill
Its purpose
The sweetness inside
Filling the space
Between our actions
And our senses-
Layers
Upon layers
Upon layers
Grown over
Our hearts
A little harder
To peel away
Help is needed
From a trusted hand
Precious nature
Revealed
Filling the space
Between our actions
And our senses
Healing the heart
Making us whole again

*There is a land that is fairer than day,
and by faith we can see it afar.*

"Sweet By and By"
Sanford Bennett

MIND'S EYE

Standing
On a shore
I've yet to see
My arms reach
My heart aches
For this place
Where sorrow
No longer exists
Where singing
Matches
The beauty
Of birds
Freely flying
On sweet
Melodies
Enveloped
By a love
So strong
There will
Never again
Be a need
To sigh
For what
Is lacking
Standing
On a shore
I've yet to see

*Blessed are those who mourn,
For they will be comforted.*

—

Matthew 5:4

SAYING GOODBYE

I did not
Understand
At the time
Still don't, really
Caused me to
Question my faith
Death often does
Especially when
Someone so young
And full of life
Faces cancer-
She fought hard
For every step
Hoped and prayed
For healing-
Looking back
I can remember
Your voice
Through the rain
That fell in rhythm
With my tears-
One week was
Not enough
But I'm thankful
We had time
To say goodbye
Even if we didn't
Speak the words

For Shannon

...we are surrounded by such
a great cloud of witnesses,
let us throw off everything that hinders...
Let us run with perseverance
the race marked out for us,
Fixing our eyes on Jesus...

—

Hebrews 12:1-2

ENDURANCE

Even the most
Detailed of maps
Must hold space
For the unexpected
Steep inclines
Sharp curves
Unrecognizable
Until imminent
Approach
A detour or two
Possibly an injury
Tempting us
To give up
On the journey-
And yet, endurance grows
Through the stories
Of all those
Running ahead
Running beside
Running behind
Moving together
Toward the one
Waiting for us
At the finish line
Ready to wrap us up
In love and celebration
Not due to our finish
But because of our faith

*And now these three remain:
faith, hope, and love.
But the greatest of these is love.*
—

1 Corinthians 13:13

TURN AWAY

Look too long
Into the mirror
And only flaws
Are magnified-
The beauty
Underneath
Waiting to shine
Shrinks, afraid
To be seen
Look too long
Into the mirror
And problems
Are magnified-
Consuming thoughts
Halting actions
Stifling the part of me
That could help
Another in need
What if I turn away from my reflection
Look into
Your loving eyes
Covered by mercy
Rescued by grace
Learning by example
Growing my faith
Loving this beautiful
But hurting world

*He hides my soul in the cleft of the rock
that shadows a dry, thirsty land.*

—

"He Hideth My Soul"
Fanny Crosby

TRY AGAIN

The drought spreads
Dry, dusty air
Into my lungs
Seeps under my skin
Hardens my heart
Oppresses my soul
I search for
A sip of water
A drop of rain
Any semblance of relief
I know it exists
That kind of help
Already at work
Before you even
Know it is needed
A light breeze
Carrying a cloud
A heavy cloud
Releasing the rain-
I try to sing
But the words
Get caught
In the back
Of my throat-
You quietly whisper
I am here. Try again
One note carries another
And soon, a melody emerges
From a time long gone
Restoring body, heart, mind, and soul

*When you pass through the waters, I will
be with you.
And when you pass through the rivers,
they will not sweep over you.*

—

Isaiah 43:2

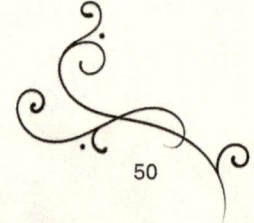

CARRIED

What seemed at first
A passing storm
Carried me out
Into the deep
Leaving me
Treading water
Barely able to
Hold my chin
Above the surface
Chest heavy
From the pressure
Arms too tired
To keep rowing
Legs too tired
To keep kicking
I could see land
In the distance
But couldn't get there
On my own strength-
Eyes closed
Fears released
In a silent prayer
Trusting
You will
Carry me
Safely back
To the shore

*...weeping may endure for a night,
but joy comes in the morning.*

—

Psalm 30:5

TAKE THEIR HANDS

Though we
Do not seek
Suffering or
Hope for sorrow
We often sense
Their approach
As when the air
Grows eerily quiet
And the sky turns
Yellowish gray
In front of an
Approaching storm
Or they may arrive
Without warning
A flash flood
Bringing instant
Devastation and
Destruction
No matter their
Method of arrival
We have a choice-
Push them away in vain
Or bravely take their hands
Walk beside them
And feel their strength
As they transform
Into joy and peace

*For I was hungry,
and you gave me something to eat.
I was thirsty,
and you gave me something to drink.
I was a stranger
and you invited me in...*

—

Matthew 25:35

LIVING KINDNESS

Thirst quenched
With a cup
Of cool water
Hunger eased
With a tasty
Morsel of food
Fears calmed
Within the warmth
Of safe shelter
Hands in desperation
Seeking to survive
Hands in kindness
Seeking to share
Hand to hand
Heart to heart
Opening doorways
Fostering pathways
Linking living souls

For we walk by faith, not by sight.

—

2 Corinthians 5:7

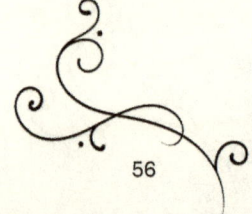

OPEN EYES

Some roads
Traveled daily
Others rarely
The everyday
Serve a purpose
Transporting from
Point A to Point B
The extraordinary
Serve a purpose
Calling only
At certain times
Carrying us to
Pinnacles
Capable of renewing
Passions dwindled
By the daily-
Paths worth traveling
Views worth beholding
Even if it means
Closing my eyes
Around steep curves
And trusting
The one in control
Will let me know
When it is safe
To open my eyes
And look around
Inviting me to see
How far I've come
And how small I am
In comparison
To the vastness
Of this world

*The light shines in the darkness,
and the darkness has not overcome it.*

—

John 1:5

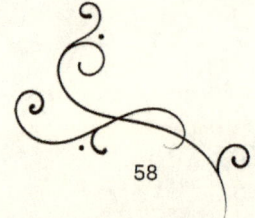

WITH HOPE

I stare into the dancing flames
Reds, yellows, oranges
Rising from the dry wood
Shifting on the ground

Fanning the playful flames
I warm my cold hands
Not too close! Flames that warm
May also burn

Extinguishing the dying flames
Water mixing with fire
I stare at the rising steam
The blackened wood

Leaving behind the cold
Leaving behind my worries
Into the light of a new day
I walk with hope

*See, I have engraved you
on the palms of my hands.
Your walls are ever before me.*

—

Isaiah 49:16

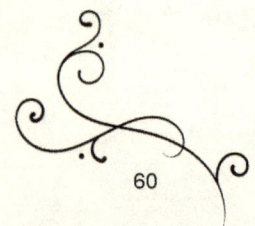

THIS ROAD

Once clear, now
Obstructed
By unexpected
Roadblocks
Detours up ahead
Which way to go?
A new road
Comes into view
Along with it
A new role
Not the one
Expected
Or desired
Yet, accepted-
Potholes trigger
Full stops...
But gentle truths
Faithfully push
Forward
Erasing any thought
Of turning back-
Moving ahead
A quiet whisper
Provides assurance-
Trust and follow
Nothing can take you
Out of my hand
Don't turn back
This road is best

*But the fruit of the Spirit is
love, joy, peace, patience, kindness,
goodness, faithfulness, gentleness, self-
control...*

—

Galatians 5:22-23

ENCOUNTER

Empty words
Of blessing
Spoken with
No action
No meaning
Have I been guilty?
Perhaps
With good intentions
But good intentions
Do not serve to
Lessen struggles
Only to ease
My discomfort
In the face of
Others' suffering
Don't let me sleep
Through their pain
Let my soul
Reflect your light
My hands
Follow your example

*Let love and kindness
be the motivation behind all that you do.*

—

1 Corinthians 16:14

BRIDGES

Conflicting
Opinions-
On one side
Shouts of anger
Worry and fear
On the other
Celebrations
Claims of victory

Caught
Somewhere
In the middle
Desperately sad
Yet, believing
There is a way
To bridge
This chasm

Life is both
Precious and
Devastatingly difficult-
Celebrating the first
Rings hollow
If I fail to
Acknowledge
The latter

Solutions
Only arrive
Covered in layers
Upon layers of love
So deep, one voice
Can neither explain
Nor take credit
For the outcome

*Let the morning bring me word
of your unfailing love,
for I have put my trust in you.*

—

Psalm 143:8

INSIDE-OUT

Clouds of bluish gray
Against a pale white
Morning sky
Felt as if
The World
Had been turned
Inside-out
Overnight-
Complete opposite
Of what my eyes
Witnessed yesterday
Bright blue sky
Crisp white clouds
Strange...
For a moment
I wondered if
Something was wrong
Was yesterday simply a cover?
Sadness hiding behind a smile?
Maybe, maybe not
A second glance
Revealed today's answer-
Morning star
Twinkling
Among the clouds
As if to say
Good morning
It's a new day
All is well
And I smiled
Not hiding
But trusting

*For everything there is a season,
and a time for every purpose under heaven.*

Ecclesiastes 3:1

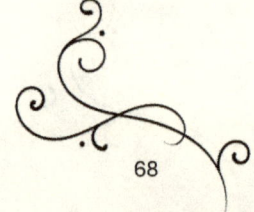

TWO SISTERS

One life begins
As another ends
The way it has
Always been
Joy and grief
Draw close
Walking
Hand in hand
Like two sisters-
I picture the two
Oil and water
Constantly at odds
Never able to
Fully resolve
Yet, they continue
On their journey
Always together
Joy reminding
Grief the reason
For her existence
Grief reminding
Joy to savor
The simple

*Even though I walk through the valley
of the shadow of death,
I will fear no evil, for you are with me.
Your rod and your staff, they comfort me.*

—

Psalm 23:4

GUARANTEE

Baby's first steps
Tentative
Uncertain
Yet, filled with
Excitement
Security
In the hands
Waiting
To grab hold
When he falls
And he will fall
Dad knows this
To be true
After all, walking
Takes practice
But eventually
Turns into running
Once again, with
A guarantee of falling-
Don't let my fear of falling
Keep me from running
Into your arms-
Believing
You will catch me

You have taken account of my wanderings.
Put my tears in Your bottle.
Are they not recorded in Your book?
—

Psalm 56:8

PRECIOUS COLLECTION

Sought after treasure
Precious stones
Rare coins
Works of art
Collected by
The highest bidder
Fattest wallet
Then hidden away
Only brought out
On special occasions
For brief display
To be fought over
In later years-
Could salty tears be so valuable?
We hold them back
Hide them from view
Dry them up
Cause them to flow
From the eyes of others-
How precious
The thought of them
Being collected
Held in a sacred vase
Written down
Never to be forgotten

*A soft and gentle and thoughtful answer
turns away wrath,
but harsh and painful and careless words
stir up anger.*

—

Proverbs 15:1

BEHIND THE SOUNDS

Yes, they are
Only words
But words
Have power
An innate ability
To change the
Trajectory
Of a day, a week,
A life...
Considering
How easily
I can be
Encouraged
Disappointed
Cheered
Saddened
By the meanings
Behind such sounds
Perhaps, I should
Choose mine
With more care
And consideration
Speaking aloud
Only the ones
I'd want to hear in return

*And the melody that He gave to me,
within my heart is ringing.*

—

"In the Garden"
Charles Austin Miles

RELEASED

I caught
A glimpse
Of you hiding
Among the leaves
Of a tall tree
Only your song
Gave you away
Each sweet note
Released with
An energy
That caused
The branches
To sway and
Leaves to rustle
Perhaps
You were not hiding
But delivering
A message meant
Just for me-

I see you
Sitting there
Hiding among
Your thoughts
Release them
I will add them
To the bird's song
And together
They will float
To the heavens

*You shall wander far in safety
though you do not know the way.*

—

"Be Not Afraid"
Robert J. Dufford

TRUSTING WANDERER

On a journey
To a place
I've never seen
Trusty map
Carefully folded
And unfolded
As needed for
Any change
In destinations
From Interstate
To scenic route
Not wanting
To miss a single
Point of interest
After all, each was
Clearly marked
In advance
But what happens
To my plan
To my faith
When a detour
Unexpectedly
Changes the route?
Do I fret?
Throw my map
Out the window?
Or trust your hand
To be my guide
Even when
I have no idea
Where I am or
Where I'm going

*For with you is the fountain of life.
In your light we see light.*

Psalm 36:9

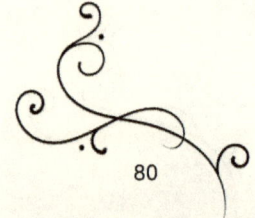

BE THE LIGHT

Experiencing
Darkness is
Universal
As is the hope
For a light
To ease
Our gloom
We are not
Intended
To live alone
On an island
No contact
With another
Living soul
Each of us
Will have
Opportunity
To be the hand
Reaching
Thru the fog
Or the one
Grateful
To be pulled
Out of the murk
Weightless
In the arms
Of our brother
Warmed in the light
Of his love

*Neither do people light a lamp
and put it under a bowl.
Instead, they put it on a stand,
and it gives light to everyone in the house.*

—

Matthew 5:15

CHILDLIKE WISDOM

This little light of mine
Cheerful words
Sung by
A child
Catchy tune
Not easily
Forgotten
Hide it under a bushel? No!
A silly question
Yet, significant
There is
A choice
Whether
To shine
Or to hide-
All around the world
Though shining
For all to see
Is not easy
Nothing and
No one has
The ability
To extinguish
My light
I'm gonna let it shine!

*Blessed are those who mourn,
for they will be comforted.*

—

Matthew 5:4

BLESSED

A puzzling word
Typically voiced
In the positive
A proud reference
To all the good
Things in life-
But what if...
We are looking
At it all wrong
What if it has
Nothing to do
With possessions
But everything
To do with
Who we are
On the inside-
A willingness
To show mercy
To show humility
To be a peacemaker
To express our grief
Accepting that true
Blessings are felt
In the stillness
Of a clear sky
Following the most
Frightening of storms

*...who made the great lights.
His love endures forever.
The sun to govern the day...*

—

Psalm 136:7-8

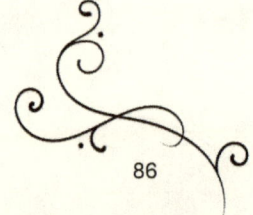

ENDURING LIGHT

Power so great
Its effects are
Seen and felt
Before it comes
Into view-
Painting
The blue
With pink
Streaks
Warming
The breeze
That blows
Thru my hair-
Spoken of
In terms of
Rising and setting
Yet, in actuality
Holds a place
Of permanence
In the heavens-
If I trust it
Will be there
With our next
Circling past
How much more
Can I trust
The One who
Placed it in the sky

*He determines the number of the stars
and calls them each by name.*

Psalm 147:4

A UNIQUE LENS

The longer I look
The more clearly I see
Those shining
Brightest
Are always
First in view
And though
Initially
Outshining
Their neighbors
All are worth
Exploring
Even when taking
A closer look
Requires a
Unique lens
One that will
Magnify light
While decreasing
The distance
Between us-
Whether gazing
Up at the stars
Or into the hearts
And souls of those
Surrounding me
A phenomenon
Of ever increasing
Light, love, and hope

*You gave me a wide place for my steps under me,
and my feet did not slip.*

—

2 Samuel 27:37

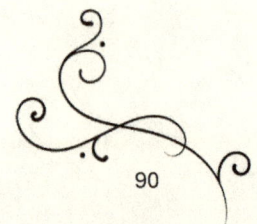

COUNTING STEPS

It begins with
The very first ones
Celebrating
As little legs
Move faster
Go farther
Grow stronger
But do I continue
Counting only for
The sake of numbers
Or contemplate
The imprints
Left behind-
There is a choice
Adjust my steps
Gentle to firm
Hasty to calm
Dependent on
Current conditions
Guided by love
Or tromp thru
Each new season
Unaware of anyone
Or anything but me
Leaving no benefit
For those following
Or walking alongside-
Accepting my steps are numbered
Making sure each one counts

...he leads me beside quiet waters.

—

Psalm 23:26

Do not wear yourself out to get rich.

—

Proverbs 23:4

GOOD TIRED

There is such
A thing
As good tired
A feeling of
Fulfillment
From working hard
Doing the right thing
Simply because
It is the right
Thing to do
Not just a goal
For reaching
The next step
On the ladder
Never-ending
Cycle of exhaustion
Dependent on approval
Of those standing by
Watching and waiting
For a fall from grace-
No, this result says
Job well-done
Time to rest
Sit beside
Quiet waters
As the sounds
Refresh the body
Calm the mind
Renew the spirit-
The continuing
Work of life
Embracing *good tired*
As its recurring theme

*Above all else, guard your heart,
for everything you do flows from it.*
—

Proverbs 4:23

HEARTBEATS

Broken hearts
Happy hearts
Both are a part
Of this life
When we feel lost
Waiting to be found
When we are found
Hoping never
To be lost again
The heart measures
Time differently
It never forgets
Being filled
Broken
Mended
Filled again
It never forgets
Growing
Loving
Beating
In sync with another
Like the tick-tock
Of the clock
Even though an
Inaccurate gauge
Where hearts
Are concerned-
Time is fluid
Holding all
The possibilities
Of the universe
Within the rhythm
Of one heartbeat

*The Lord is the stronghold of my life,
of whom shall I be afraid?*

—

Psalm 27:1

*As water reflects the face,
so one's life reflects the hearts.*

—

Proverbs 27:19

FACES OF WATER

Reflections
In a mountain lake
Fluffy white clouds
Floating above
High peaks
Surrounded by
Clear blue sky
A child stands
On the mossy bank

Erosion
In pillars of rock
Layers of color
A landscape
Ever-changing
With the falling
And the rising
Of formidable
Flood waters

Refreshment
In steady rain
Falling from
The clouds
Reviving the Earth
Washing away
The dust
A reminder
Of our salvation

There is no fear in love.
But perfect love drives out fear.
—

1 John 4:18

HIDING

Arms crossed
Head down
Hurts buried deep
No longer
Waiting
For a sign
An honest smile
Extended hand
That might have
Renewed hope

Fingers pointed
Judgment passed
Without asking
A single question
Showing sympathy
Could shine light
On past mistakes
Breaking an image
That took years
To create

Both are hiding
Out in the open
Missing the
Opportunity
To know peace
That comes
By letting go
To know love
That heals
Broken hearts

*A gossip betrays a confidence,
but a trustworthy person keeps a secret.*

—

Proverbs 11:13

TRUSTWORTHY

How much is
A secret worth?
Held over a head
The cost is great
A chest filled with
Worry and regret
Fear it will escape
The mouth of
The one who
Never should
Have held it-
If only it had
Been shared instead
With the tiny sparrow
Transformed into a
Forgiving melody
And carried away
With the breeze
Most certainly
The Sparrow
Would have been
A better choice

*Because of the Lord's great love,
we are not consumed,
for his compassions never fail.
They are new every morning.
Great is your faithfulness.*

—

Lamentations 3:22-23

HEARTFELT CONFESSION

I used to be good
At pretending
Always wearing
A smile to cover
Any hint of a problem
An illusion of control
Over a life headed
In the wrong direction
Lured into
Taking a detour
By words dripping
Of flattery and praise
Later paired with
Insults and threats
A whiplash
Leaving me confused
Filled with guilt
And shame
I used to be good
At pretending
Until I learned
To ignore
Hollow words
And embrace
The compassion
Found only
In words of
Truth and grace
A love unconditional

*May the God of hope fill you
with all joy and peace
as you trust in him,
so that you may overflow with hope
by the power of the Holy Spirit.*

—

Romans 15:13

QUIET EMBERS

Peace camps
Alongside joy
Inseparable
Like quiet embers
Continually glowing
In the darkness-
On occasion
Smoke from
Fires raging
Uncontrolled
Temporarily
Blocks them
From view
And fear that
They may have
Vanished
In the flames
Attempts to creep in
But if I sit still
Listening well
Memories of
Their presence
In times past
Ease my fears
And I am able
To hear their
Present message

We are still here
We will never leave

And my thoughts
Wander back
To the fire
In my soul
Once again
Warming my heart

ABOUT THE AUTHOR

Kelley Morris grew up west of Little Rock, Arkansas, a few miles from the beautiful Pinnacle Mountain State Park. She began playing piano as a young girl and earned her bachelor's and master's degrees in piano performance and collaboration. Kelley and her husband reside in Oklahoma, where they raised their three children. Kelley loves writing poetry that helps her connect with others.

www.ingramcontent.com/pod-product-compliance
Lightning Source LLC
Chambersburg PA
CBHW020013050426
42450CB00005B/450